HOW TO PROPOSE TO YOUR GIRLFRIEND

25 OF THE BEST AND MOST CREATIVE WAYS TO POP THE QUESTION

SAMANTHA EVANS

ONE
INTRODUCTION

This book is a quick and helpful guide for men (or women) who can't decide how to "pop the question". It covers all kinds of marriage proposals from simple and traditional to completely "ballsy" non- traditional approaches.

It also goes into detail about how it can happen or what would need to take place for it to happen. The ideas are creative and will completely melt her heart and make the proposal unforgettable. It will be a proposal that she will be proud to tell her friends how you "popped the question".

Enjoy!

THE POWER OF FOOD

Placing the diamond ring in a chocolate cake and waiting for your girl to take a bite until she gets a rather unexpected surprise – sweet, but a little bit ancient. Your girlfriend probably saw that move already in a Hollywood high school drama or a chic-flick. Proposing nowadays is more than just dropping the "Will you marry me?" part. It is now more focused on being thoughtful and romantic, especially now that social media plays a role in everybody's lives. Of course, having her say "Yes!" is the most important part of the deed, but these days, the big question is "Was it worth Instagraming?" or "Will she post this on Facebook?" or even post a shout out on 'Twitter"?

Women in nature are tender and warmhearted. They easily fall for surprises, big or small. Her memories as a kid were probably about princes and princesses, fairies and wonderlands, and she grew up dreaming that one day she will have her own happily ever after. It is now up to you, as the (hopefully) soon-to-be fiancée, whether you will make her fairytale proposal come true or burst her dream bubble.

You need to make your proposal unique and memorable because you will only be doing this once in your entire life. Here are 25 ways to pop the question and make her say yes.

If you both share a passion for food feasts, buffet weeknights, or Sunday food bazaars, she would probably love a proposal involving your common denominator, which is food.

1. Why don't you take a crash course on baking and learn how to make customized cupcakes with her favorite flavors? Everything with a personal touch is engaging. Women are suckers for these pastries ever since Carrie Bradshaw appeared with them in Sex and the City. A dozen cupcakes decorated with edible roses and fondant letters is a promising concept that you can use. And instead of writing "Will you marry me?" come up with something more personal like for example, "Grow old with me."

Deliver the box right at her doorstep on a random night, or simply tell her after dinner that dessert is on you. It could probably be a bit tacky, but once your girlfriend finds out that you learned to bake just for proposing to her, then it would be pretty hard for her to say "no". You earn a skill, plus you win her heart, it's a win-win situation. Remember, guys that bake are rare and women love to be associated with something (or someone) that no one else has.

2. If you both enjoy watching movies on your free nights, or snuggling in front of the TV when you don't feel like going out, a really surprising way of popping the question is placing it at the bottom of the tub of fries or popcorn. Choose a really moving and romantic movie with a happy ending to help set up the mood for your proposal, she might even think it's sweet that you chose that kind of movie instead of the usual action and horror flicks that you prefer. The real ending is not the show itself, but the message at the bottom of your snack tub. Just make sure she gets the last handful of your popcorn and prepare to go down on one knee.

3. Not a movie-buff? You could instead treat her to a fancy meal at your favorite buffet restaurant. The thing with buffets is that you get to enjoy choosing your favorite dishes over a wide array of other food in a very long table. To set up your proposal, ask the chefs and crew to set aside a chafing dish for you. Position a plate inside with the message "Marry me!" written in melted chocolate together with a special box for the diamond ring.

Place the dish where you know she would go last. It would most likely be the desserts area. Ask your accomplices to set it up for you once you think she's ready for dessert. You may also try to convince her to open the chafer by saying that it's your new personal favorite, but make it casual so it would not be too obvious.

TWO

USING THE GREAT OUTDOORS

4. Proposing on the beach with that romantic sunset or sunrise backdrop is fantastic. But remember, you don't want it to be a "That's it?" kind of thing. Add up some flair and kick up the excitement by asking her to go parasailing.

Soar high into the clouds and ask her to marry you while you are a hundred or so feet in the air. Just make sure that the ring will not fall into the water as you propose. Have it securely strapped onto you and pop up the question while you two are airborne. Chances are, you would be landing by the sea and walking back to shore romantically engaged.

5. However, if you prefer something that will not hype up your adrenaline and instead create a simpler and romantic mood, bring her to a romantic beach getaway and casually build sand castles and collect shells with your love. Place your diamond ring inside a shell and place it on top of the sandcastle that you two built and then ask her to open the shell. Include the message "Be my queen forever. Will you marry me?" It may sound spontaneous, so make sure that you propose on the perfect timing.

6. Another idea of a romantic wedding proposal is to surprise her in the morning. Rent a beach house with the perfect shoreline. Before she wakes up, write your message on the sand. You may do it with small rocks and shells, or you may write directly on the sand using a twig. Just make sure that the water will not wash it away. Write your proposal legibly; that the moment she wakes up to drink her cup of coffee on the veranda and breathe in some fresh air, it would be the first thing that she would notice. Just as she sees your message, smile at her and present her with the diamond ring.

THREE

GIVING HER AN ADRENALINE RUSH

It sounds bizarre having to propose for marriage while you are experiencing an intense adrenaline rush. Creating a whole new atmosphere of fun and excitement with the thought of proposing memorably could be a little eccentric in some ways, but it can also be somewhat romantic as well.

7. Ask her out for an adventure-filled vacation and then try bungee jumping. It might be a whole new experience for the both of you, but what makes it extra special is popping the question with a banner reading "I would free-fall 233 meters above the ground just to marry you." Of course bringing the diamond ring with you as you are coiled from above, hanging upside down, may not be a good idea so just leave it on the ground with your other gear. You may present the ring right after you get through that harrowing, yet exhilarating experience. Just make sure that your girlfriend is ready for this kind of extreme adventure, because you wouldn't want your soon-to-be fiancée fainting right in the middle of your proposal, right?

8. Another new sport, less dangerous than bungee

jumping is "Zorbing". It is a sport where in you are positioned securely inside a huge, plastic orb, harnessed or not, rolling downhill on a gentle slope. Why is it romantic? Imagine you are in a huge bubble, with just you and her. It is absolutely the perfect experience.

FOUR
KEEPING IT SIMPLE

9. You may choose to propose outside the ordinary, but on the other hand, you may also be that laid-back kind of guy. Simple, but classy – like taking her out on a candlelit dinner; this might not be an outrageous and YouTube worthy approach, but it is never out of the record.

10. A trip to the park would also be a nice gesture. You may go for the conventional picnic with snacks in a basket, or you can set-up a romantic mood with a bottle of champagne, coupled with a box of chocolates, as you lay hand-in-hand enjoying the serenity around you. As you watch the clouds go by, tell her how much she means to you and how you see your future with her. Then simply slip the ring on her finger and ask her to be yours forever.

11. You can also take her to a fireworks show where you could have dinner while enjoying the breathtaking light show painting the night skies. Kiss her during the finale and pop the question as the background music takes away the night.

12. Another idea is to make her breakfast in bed. A very charming latte art on her cup of cappuccino is really allur-

ing. Add in a stack of her favorite pancakes, or an omelet personally prepared by you, a bouquet of roses, and a small package of diamond ring for breakfast sounds instantly lovely.

13. If by chance you and your girlfriend enjoy riding in a boat or canoe, you should ask her out for a ride. Paddle your way to a romantic backdrop of the river or lake and ask her hand in marriage. Another, rather expensive idea is to take her to Venice, enjoy the romance in the air, ride a gondola, ask the boatman to sing a romantic background song, kiss your girl and seize the moment. If a trip outside the country is too costly, probably a dinner or lunch at a yacht would suit her preferences. Take her breath away with the help of the sea and ask her to be your wife.

14. The ideas are endless. You could even bring back the kid in you and try the things that you used to love doing. Bring her to your local theme park and propose up high while riding a Ferris wheel. You could also take her to a magic show and hire the magician as your proposal accomplice. Make sure that your girl will be called up the stage to participate and make sure that she gets the message. Request your magician to set-up the magic tricks for you. Instead of pulling out a rabbit out of a hat, pull out three red roses. Then, perform the coin trick, but instead of a penny, make the diamond ring appear behind her ear. She is probably as to why the magic show is going the way it is, and at this point you should ask her for her hand in marriage by putting up a sign from your seats in the audience with the message, "You make my life magical. Will you marry me?"

15. Likewise, the place where you first met is also an ideal place to propose. Rekindle the memories as you walk through the lobbies and grounds of your old university. Buy her a drink at your favorite Saturday night hangouts. Remi-

nisce your first date and everything that you've been through together and declare your proposal by telling her how you would love to open a new chapter of your love story.

You may also relax together at a spa or a massage parlor. While you are enjoying the calmness of the place, whisper your proposal to her ears and slip the ring on her finger.

FIVE
USING MUSIC TO YOUR ADVANTAGE

16. There are a lot of couples that are into arts and are both musically inclined. This is your chance to make full use of your talents and creativity; compose a heartfelt song for your girl and use it in your proposal. Gather up the courage to perform it in front of her live at the right place and at the right time. You may choose to jam with a set of friends or go solo.

17. Invite your girl to the theater to watch a show. Beforehand, discuss your plans with the cast members and the people behind the play. At the end of the production, create a curtain call by having one of the actors call your darling up stage and proclaim your grand proposal in front of the casts and its audience.

18. Do you like attending concerts? Buy front-row tickets for two for the show of a boy band that she's been crushing on, or an international pop idol, or just a local band playing in your favorite bar. Tell the crew about how your girlfriend would love to go backstage and propose to her with the help of her favorite stars. She wouldn't just be

star-struck, but also romantically dazed with how her night ended.

19. However, if having a superstar witness your proposal seems impossible, then be the star yourself. Organize a karaoke party with a couple of your friends. Set the mood and tell them ahead. That way, your friends would be willing to create a more intimate atmosphere when you think the perfect time to surprise her has come. Sing a song especially dedicated for her and declare your proposal at the end of the song. Present your engagement ring and kneel in front of her saying, "I'm sorry Justin Bieber could not come here tonight. But the show must go on, so here I am asking for your hand in marriage. Be mine forever baby!"

SIX
HI-TECH IDEAS

20. A photo-collage with a solo photo of you holding a sign board at the middle could be creative. The question is where to place it? While your girlfriend is asleep, grab her tablet or mobile phone and change the wallpaper. Set the romantic mood by changing her alarm tone into her favorite love song. When she wakes up, she would notice the difference and would instantly grab her mobile or her tablet. Make sure to put sweet photos of you together as a couple on your collage and not embarrassing photos of her when she was still chubby in high school. It could be a photo of you on your first date or a photo on Valentine's Day, or the first time you went out of town together. Be creative.

21. You could also create a wicked proposal video on YouTube or Vimeo. Casually tell her that you found an insanely funny video clip and send the link to her if you are both in different locations. If you are together though at the moment, ask her to sit on your lap and invite her to watch a "new movie trailer". Make sure to propose directly as your heart says. You may quote a part of a poem or a song and

add your own words at the end. Take note that this should be something she would be proud to share on her social network. It should be something memorable and sweet that you could choose to play at your own wedding reception.

SEVEN
GOING BIG

Nothing would make your soon-to-be fiancée more comfortable but celebrating a momentous occasion with her own circle. It may be her friends, her family, her work mates or simply a group of common people that you both share.

22. You can throw a surprise party for her birthday and invite the people she is closest with. Then again, you just have to make sure to invite the same people to your wedding to avoid the stress of misunderstanding. A casual cocktail party sounds like a good idea. Situate the event in an area where you and the guests could mingle with each other. Consider the number of people invited, as these are the same people who would witness you and your soon-to-be fiancée as you walk down the aisle. Throughout the party, tell them that you have a huge announcement to make. Ask her to stand right at the middle of her family and friends and greet her with a "Happy Birthday!" as she thanks you for your admiring thoughts about her, kneel down and propose to her. You could probably start with, "I could not think of a better timing than your special day. I want to make it extra special by asking for your hand in marriage."

23. Alternatively, you can opt for a more intimate occasion by making the announcement simple. Reserve a table for a minimum for five or ten people at your favorite fine dining restaurant and celebrate with her family and best friends over dinner. It may be your favorite Italian restaurant, her favorite sushi bar, or your favorite go-to western bistro as a couple. The cuisine does not matter. However, make the announcement when you think everybody is prepared, not when her father is busy cracking a lobster open or when her best friend takes her time in the wash room; propose to her when everyone is ready and present at the table

24. This next bit will require a lot of careful planning and the cooperation of you and your girlfriend's family. You need the help of a lot of people because you will be inciting a flash mob performance. There's this one viral video of a guy recruiting his soon-to-be in-laws to help him with his proposal; they danced and lip-synced to the tune of Bruno Mars' "Marry You", and needless to say, the girl said yes. This would require a lot of careful planning and plenty of practice to get right, not to mention that you have to do all of these without your girlfriend finding out. Choreograph your flash mob to dance to her favorite song, and give it your own little twist and then pop the question at the end of the song. Although this kind of engagement would be very difficult to pull off, it would be very memorable and it would also be pretty hard for her to say "no" when you pop the question in the end.

25. If dancing however is not your talent, then might as well take her to where her dreams began and be her prince charming. Take her to Disneyland; because everybody loves going to Disneyland. Make it spontaneous yet romantic at the same time. Enjoy the day with her family or your family

and wait for the fireworks display at midnight. She's probably exhausted with all the rides, and the site seeing, but certainly it was a blissful day for both of you. End the night with the fireworks display and take the background music "A Whole New World" as a queue. The music never fails to uplift someone's spirits so pop the question by starting with, "Since this is the place where dreams come true, would you make mine come true tonight?" Have someone to take a video as you propose so you have something to remember this moment.

AFTERWORD

Whatever approach you choose, whoever you invite with you, the most important part is remembering why you are proposing to the girl of your dreams. You are expressing your love for her, which you will share for a lifetime; it is not about how tacky, or how crazy, or how surprised she was when you ask the question. The truth is you are creating a part of your love story where you are the star. OWN IT! After the proposal, prepare for another joy ride of having an engagement party and planning for your wedding.

www.ingramcontent.com/pod-product-compliance
Lightning Source LLC
Chambersburg PA
CBHW070800040426
42333CB00060B/1722